FUN ROBOT COLORING BOOK FOR KIDS

Sky Ice Johan Publication ©2015
SkyIceJohan@gmail.com

Publisher's Note: This is a work of fiction. Names, characters, places, and incidents are a product of the author's imagination. Locales and public names are sometimes used for atmospheric purposes. Any resemblance to actual people, living or dead, or to businesses, companies, events, institutions, or locales is completely coincidental.

Ordering Information:

Quantity sales. Special discounts are available on quantity purchases by corporations, associations, and others. For details, contact the "Special Sales Department" at the address above.

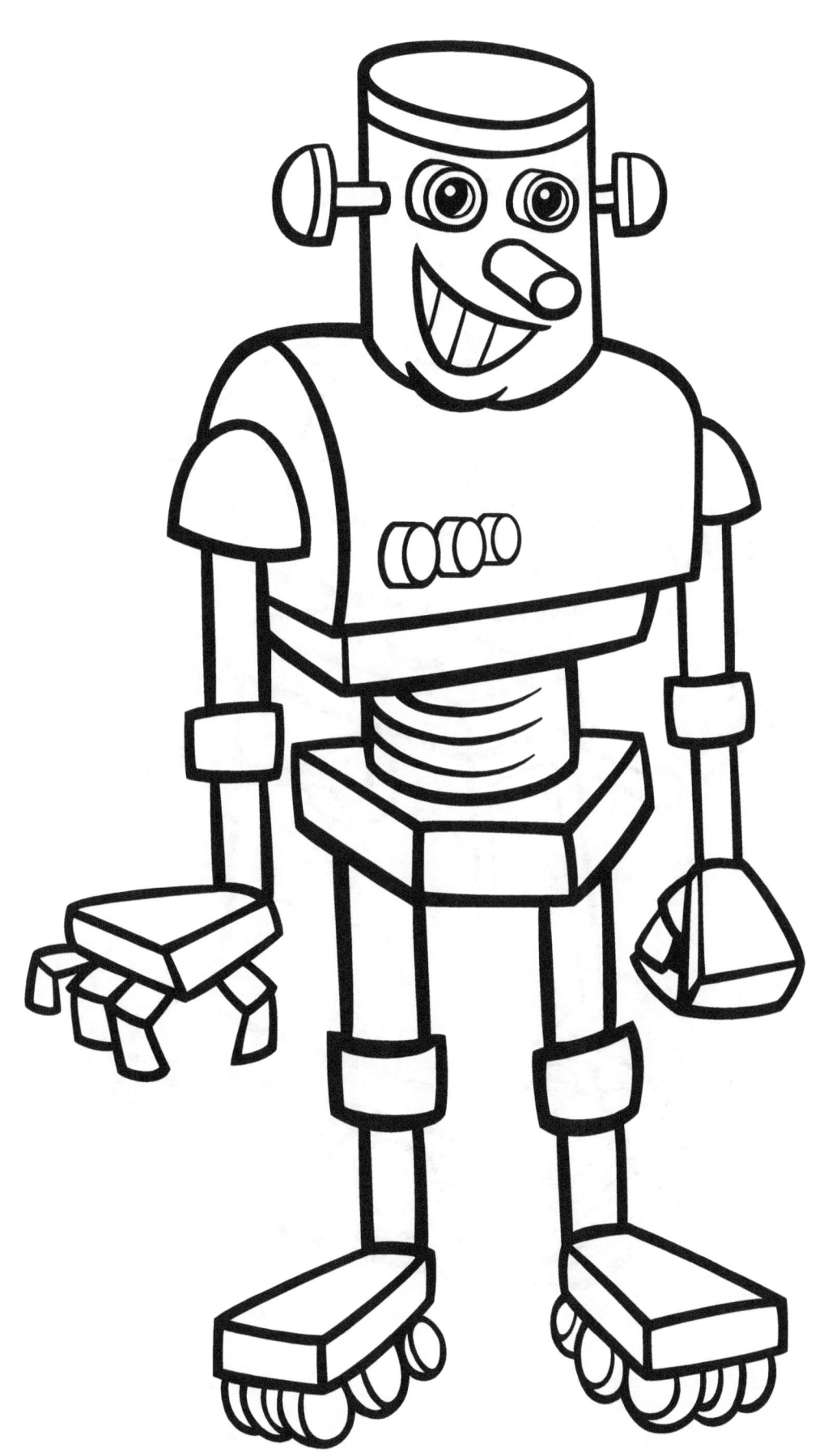

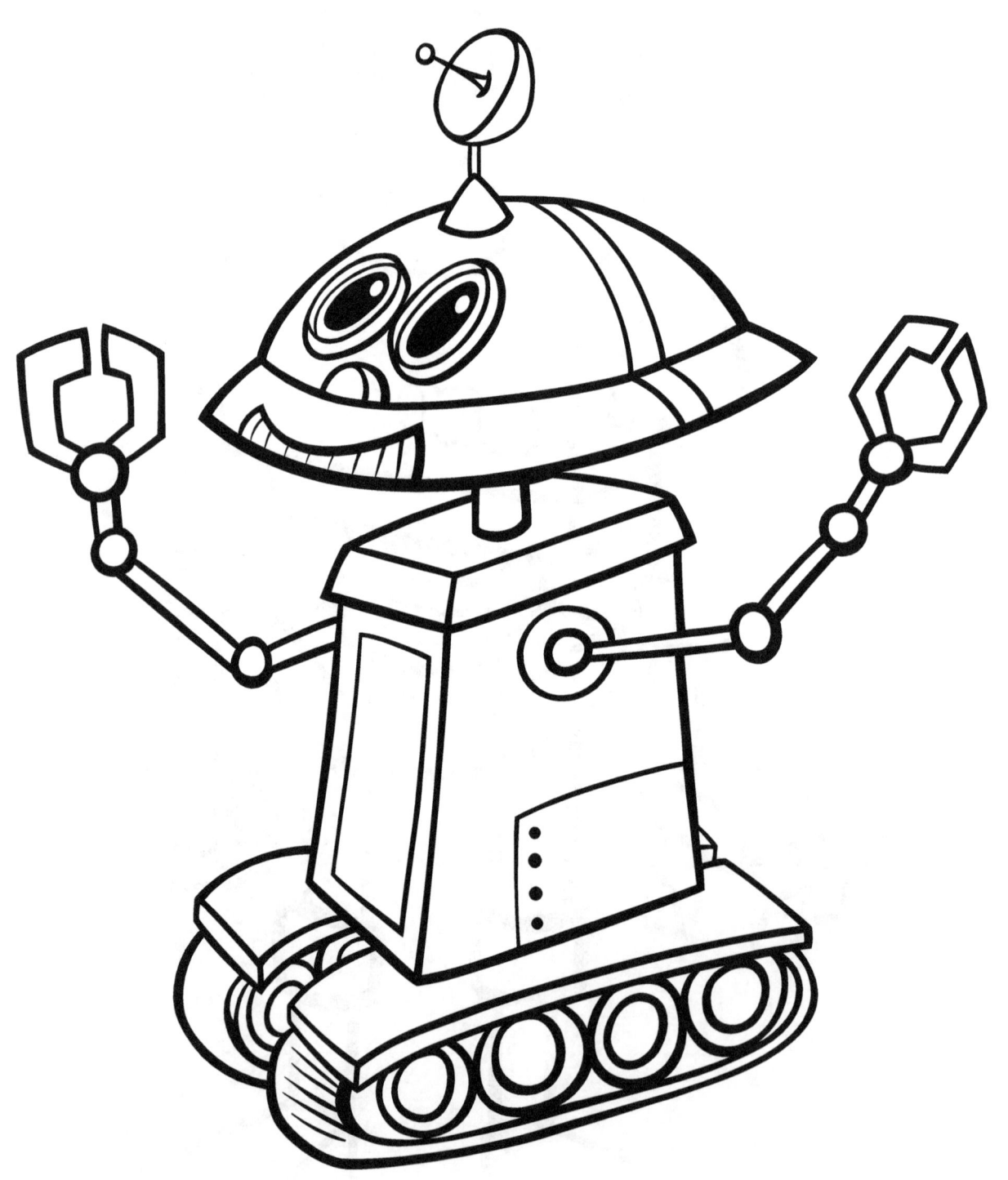

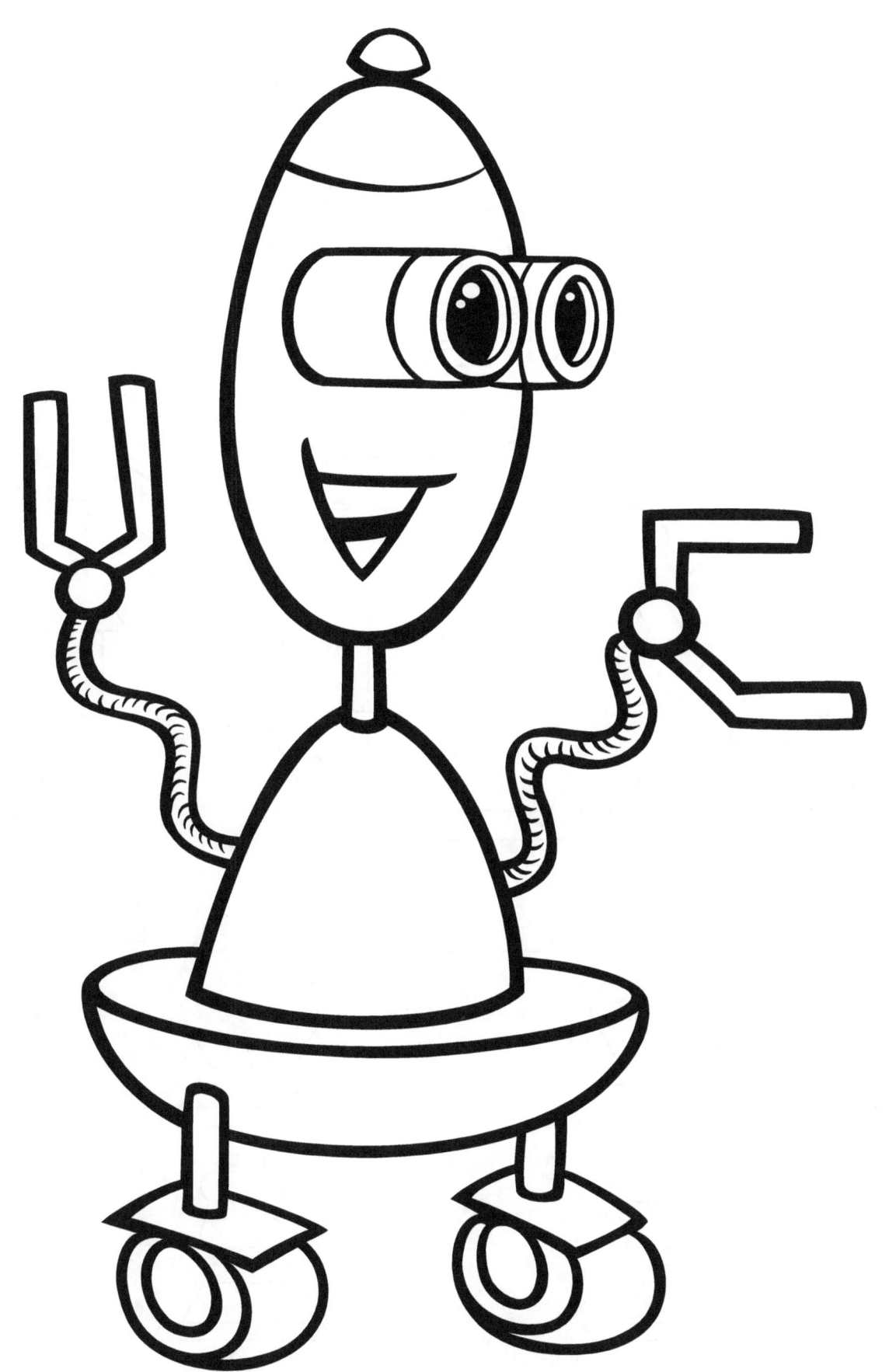

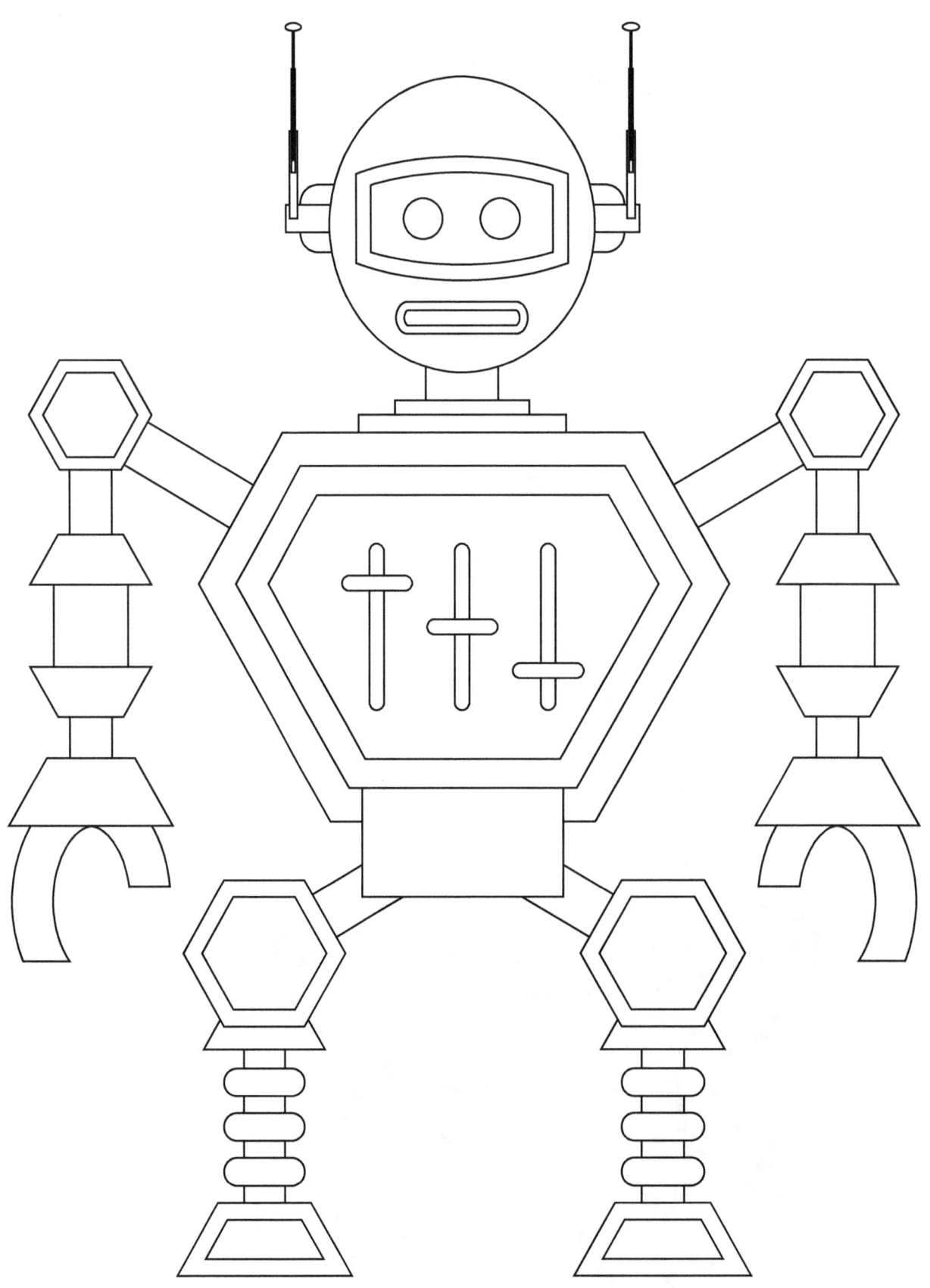

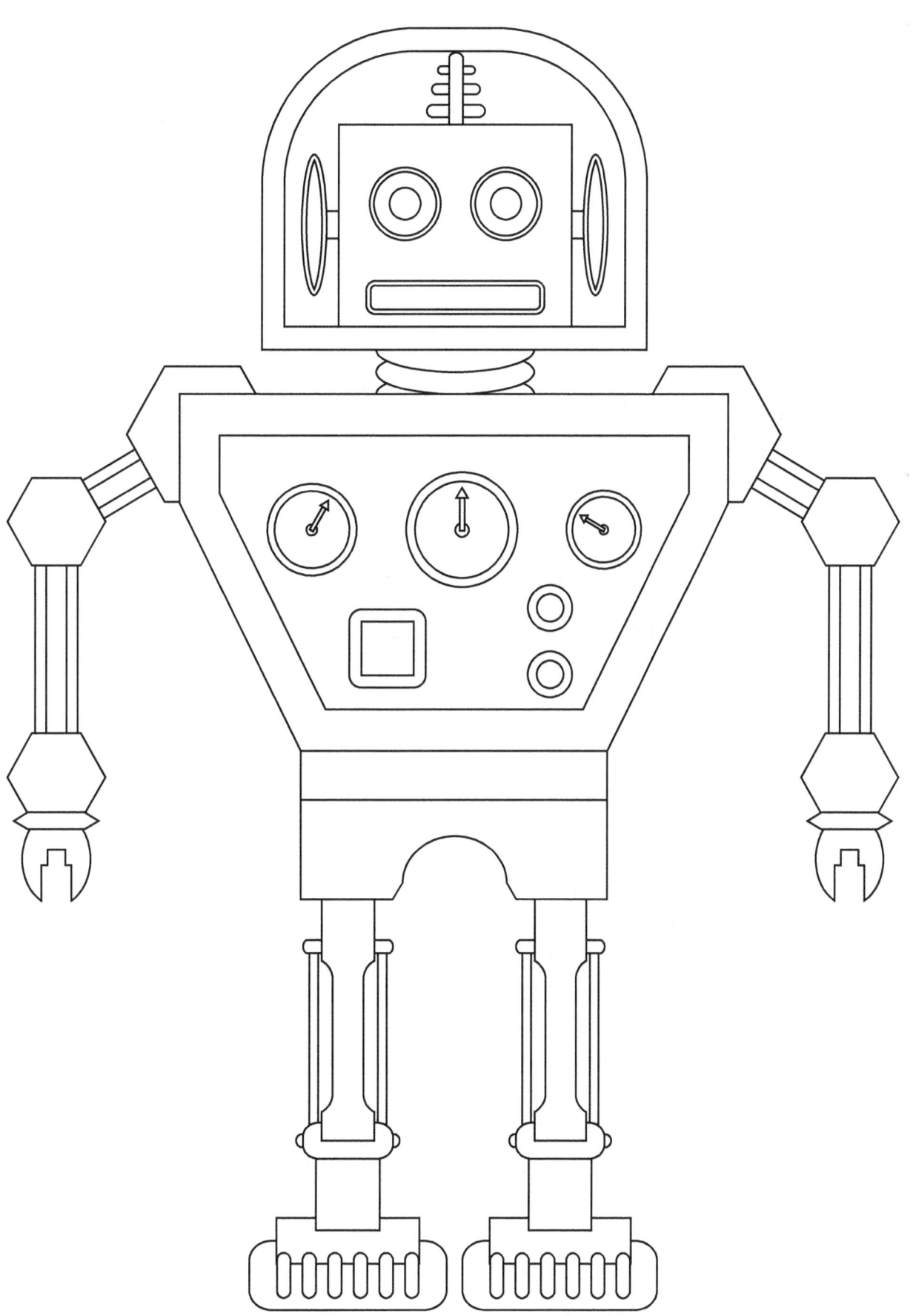

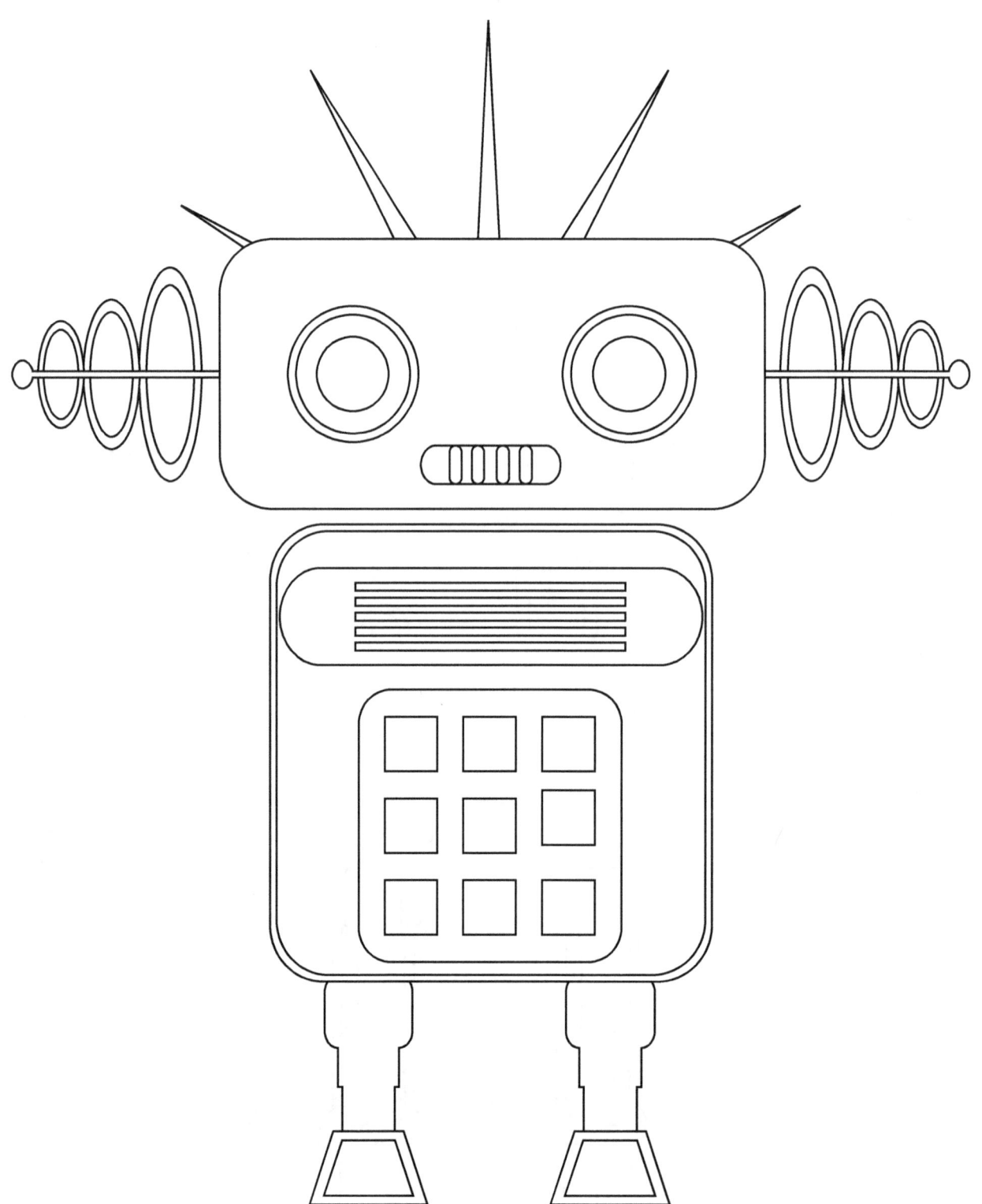

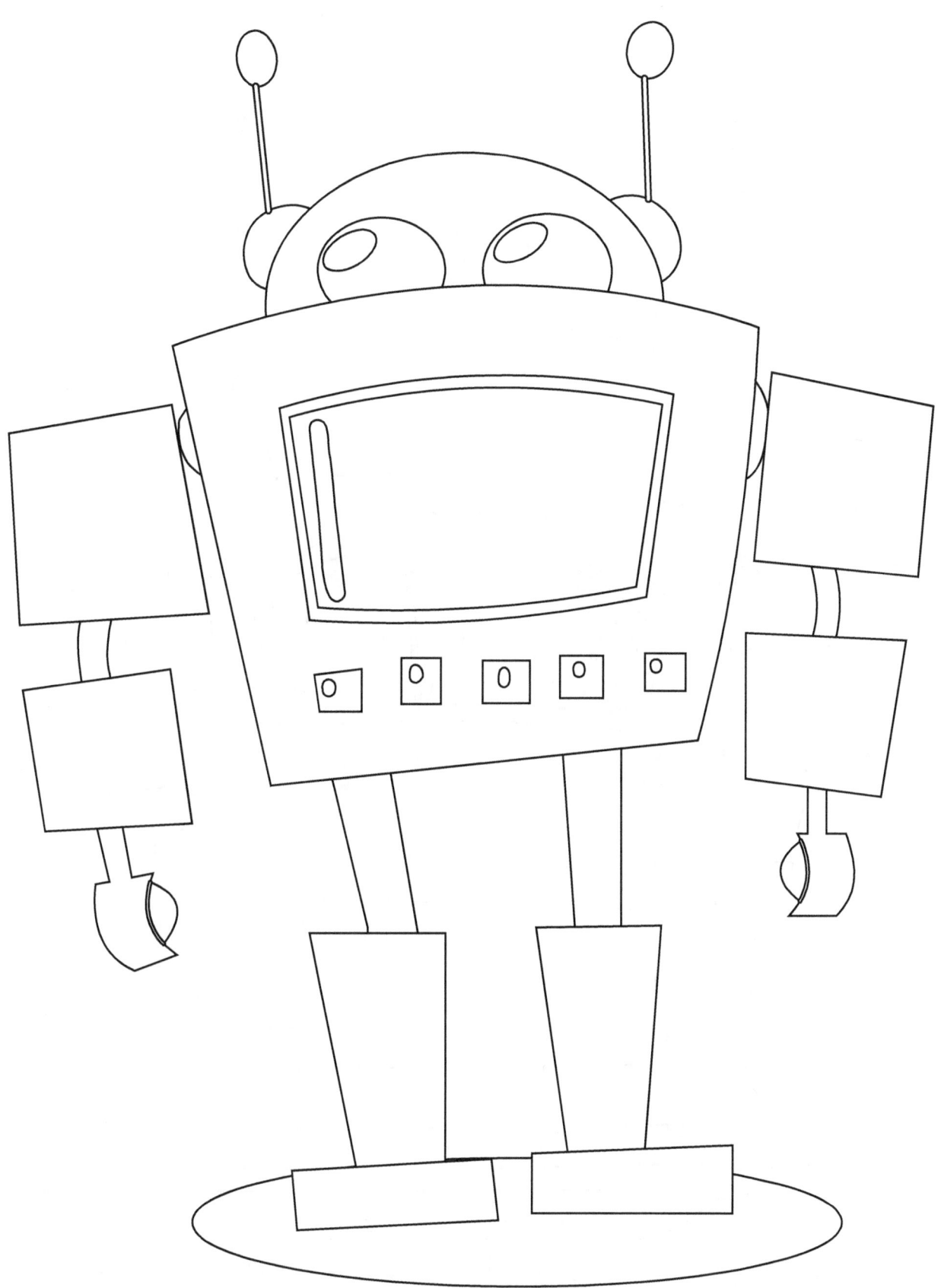

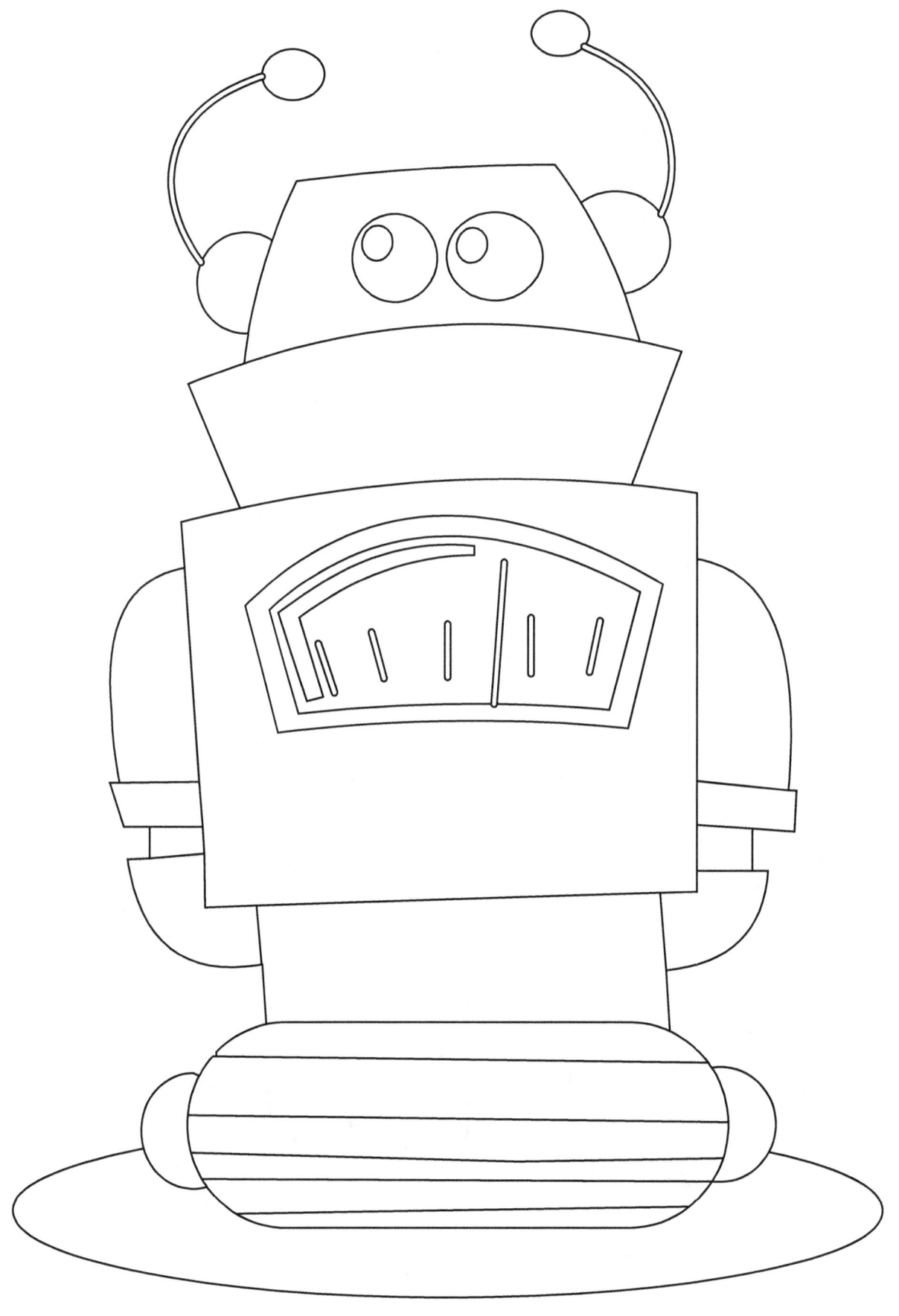

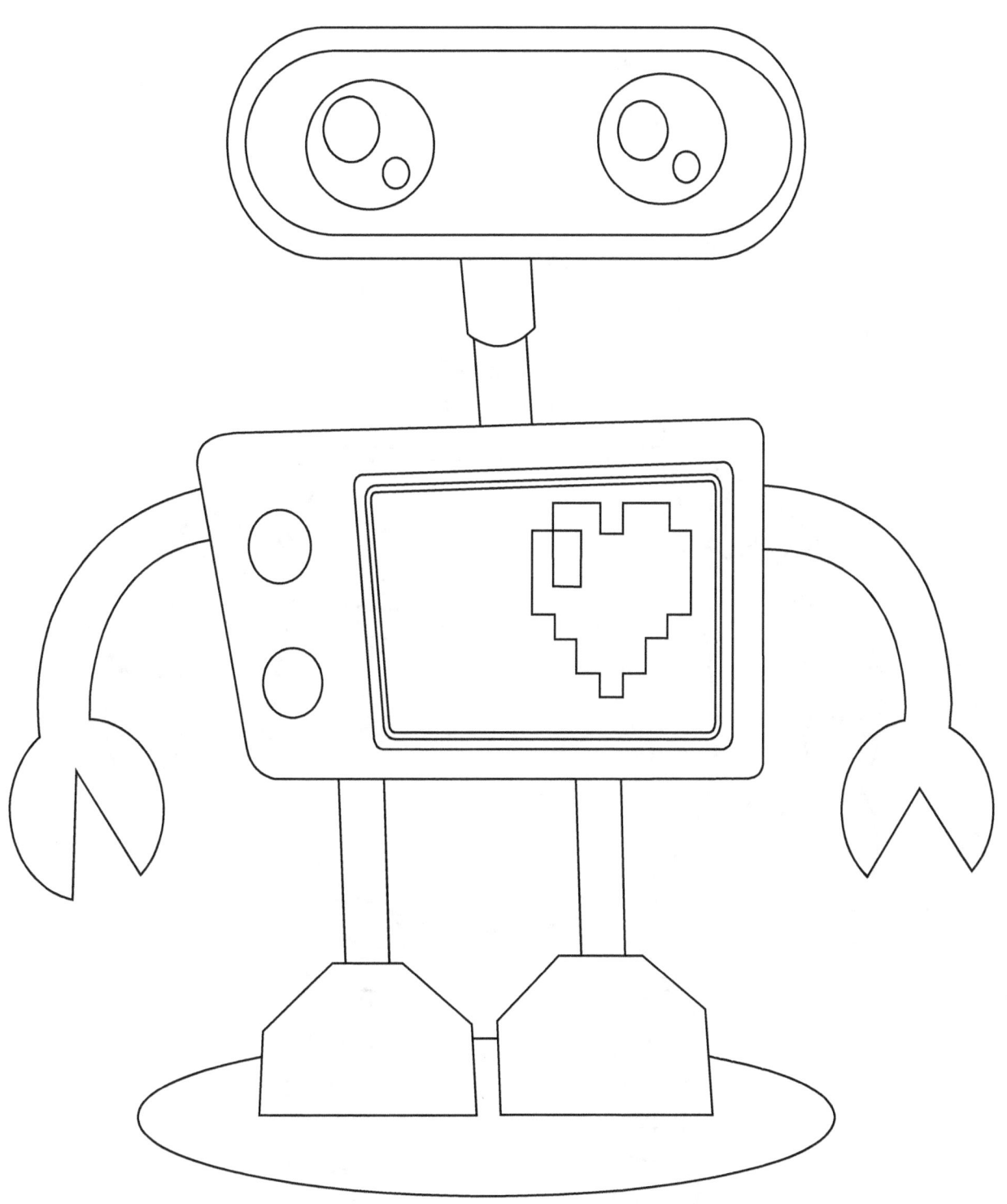

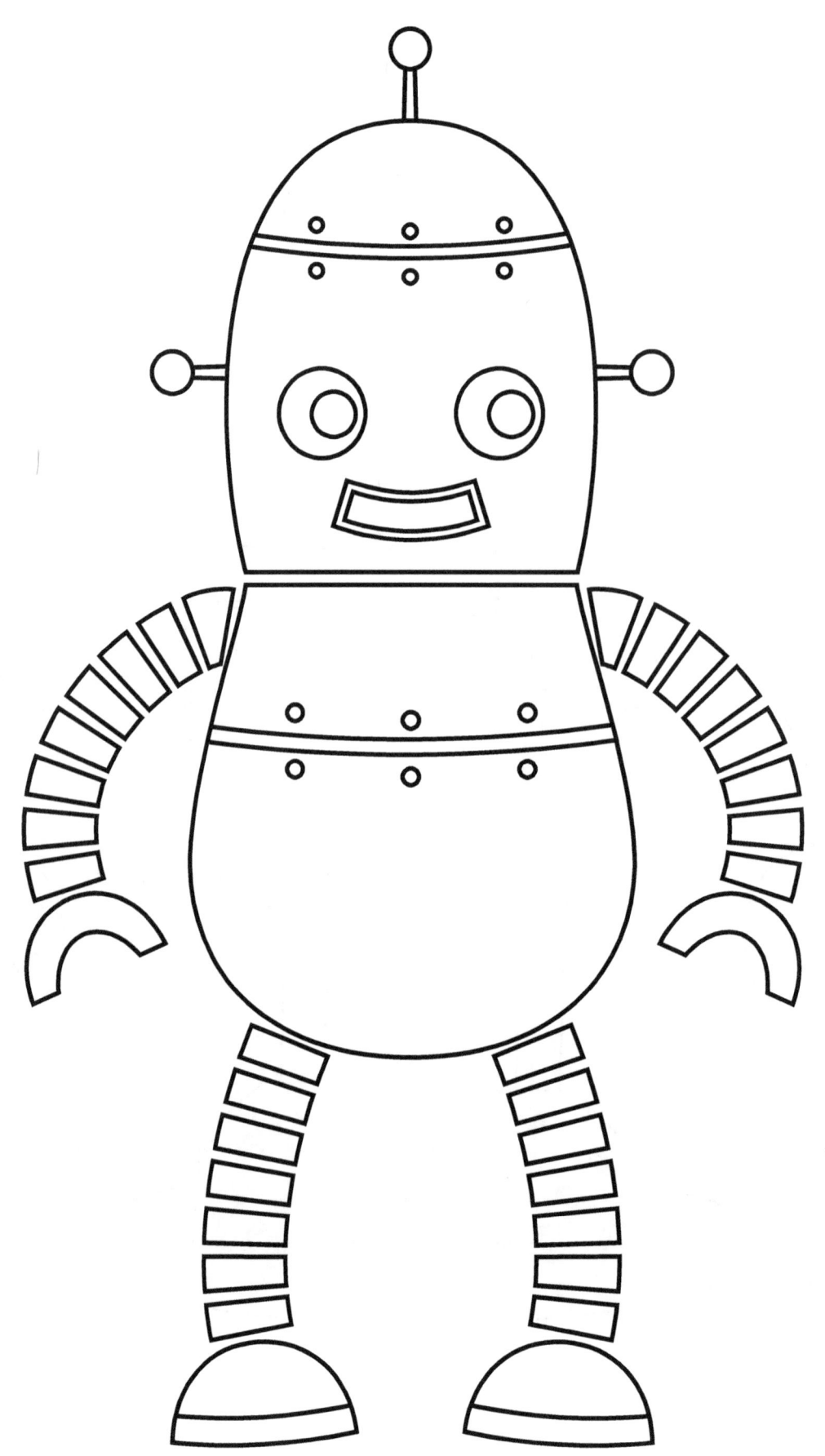

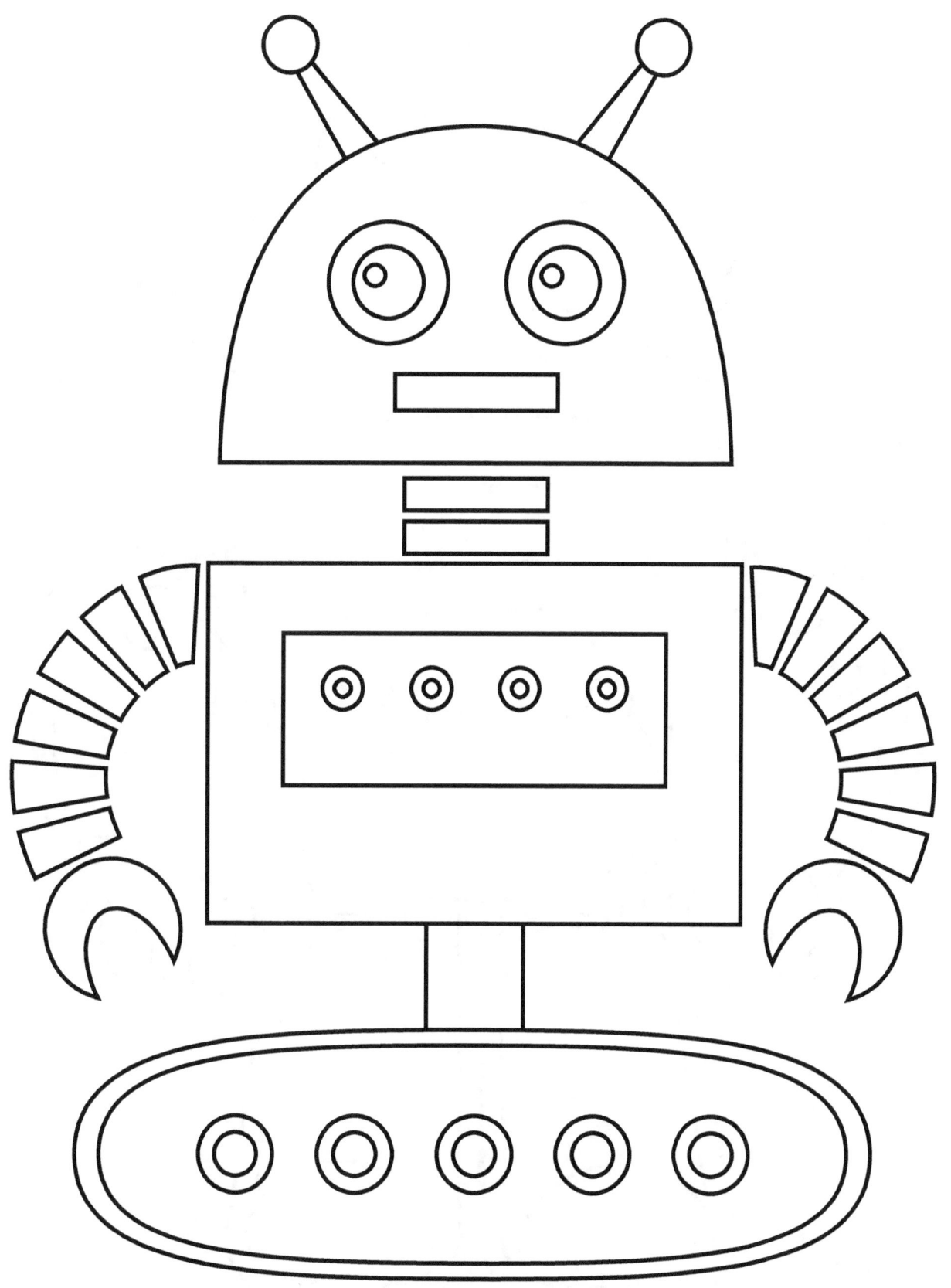

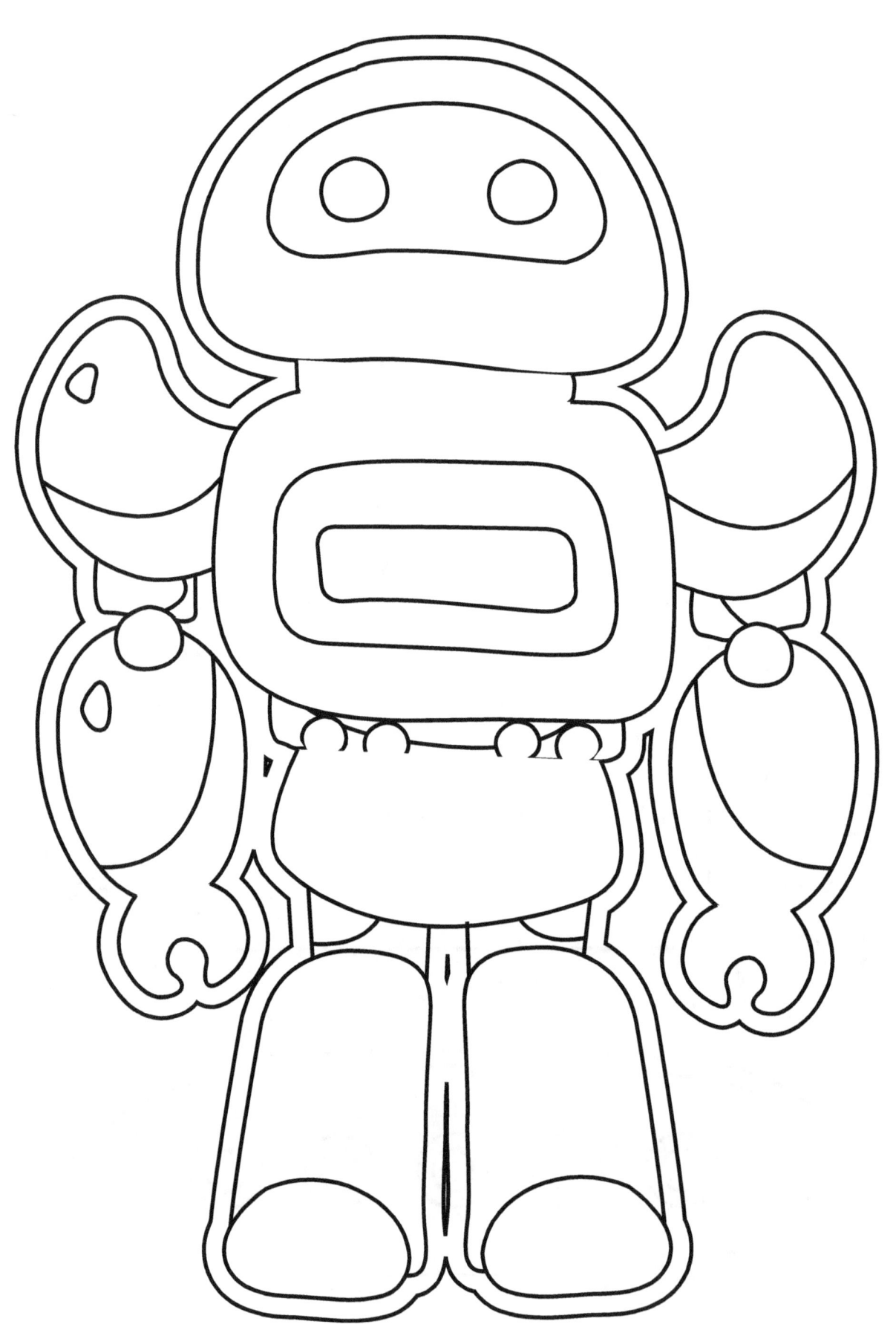

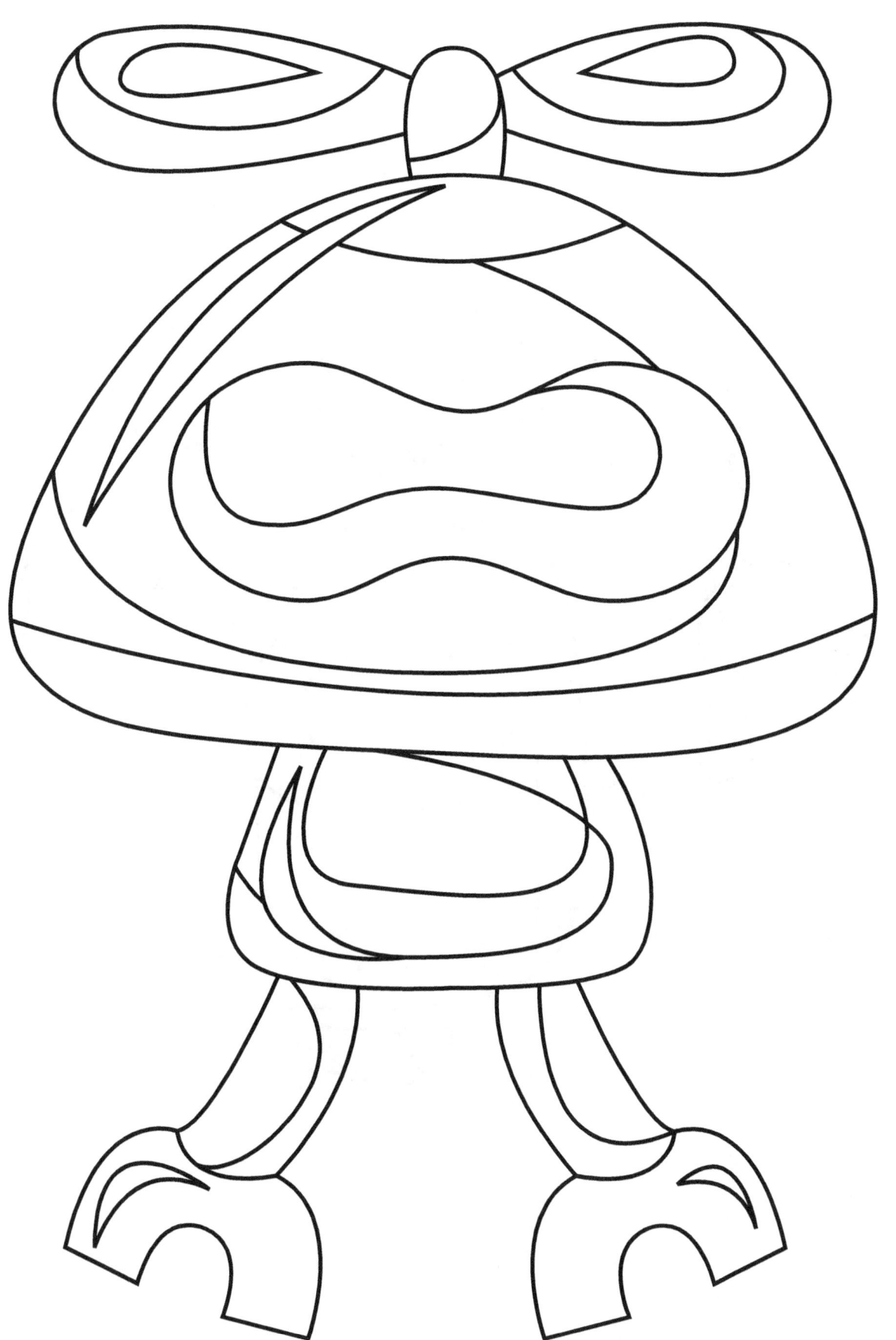

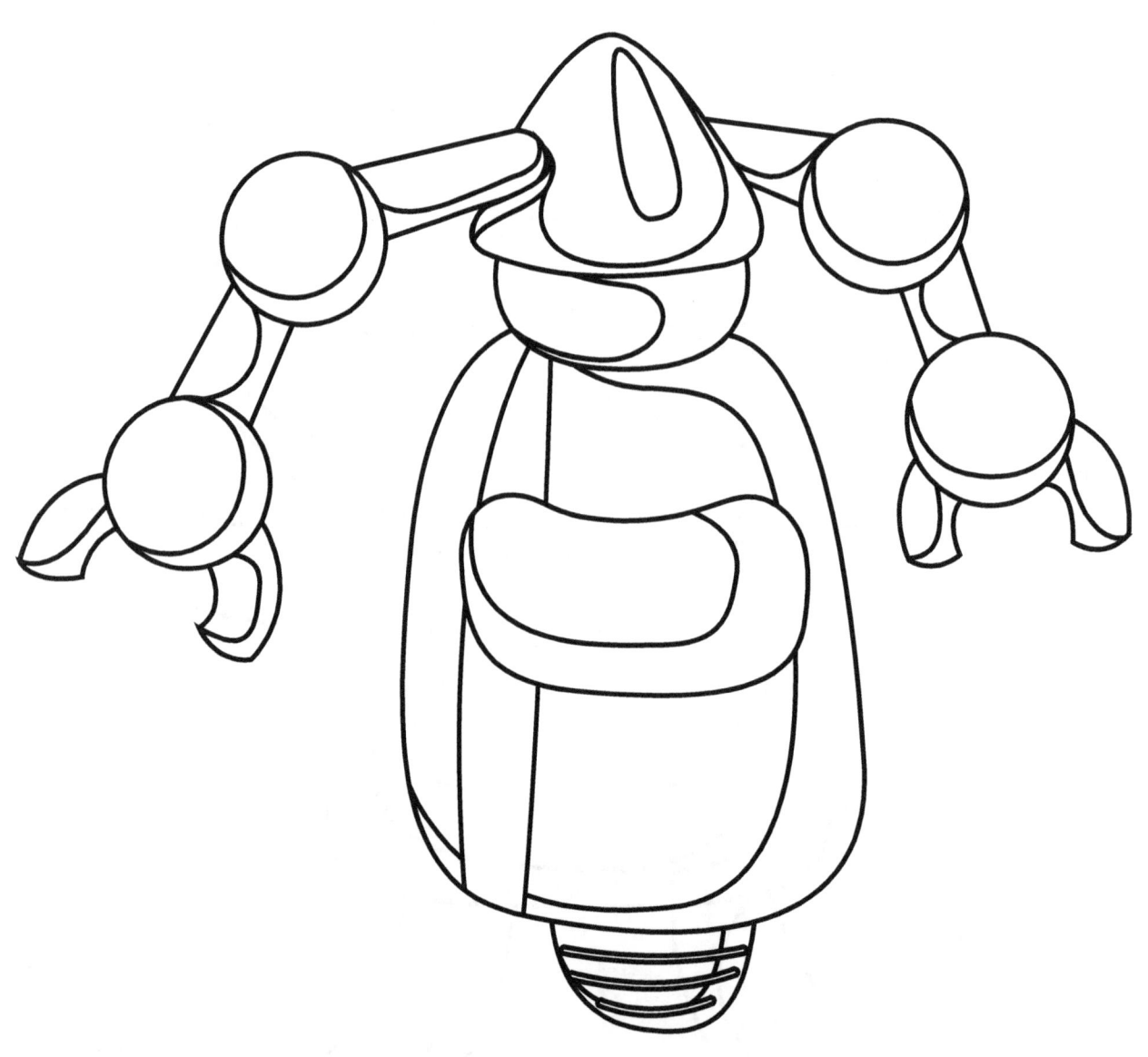

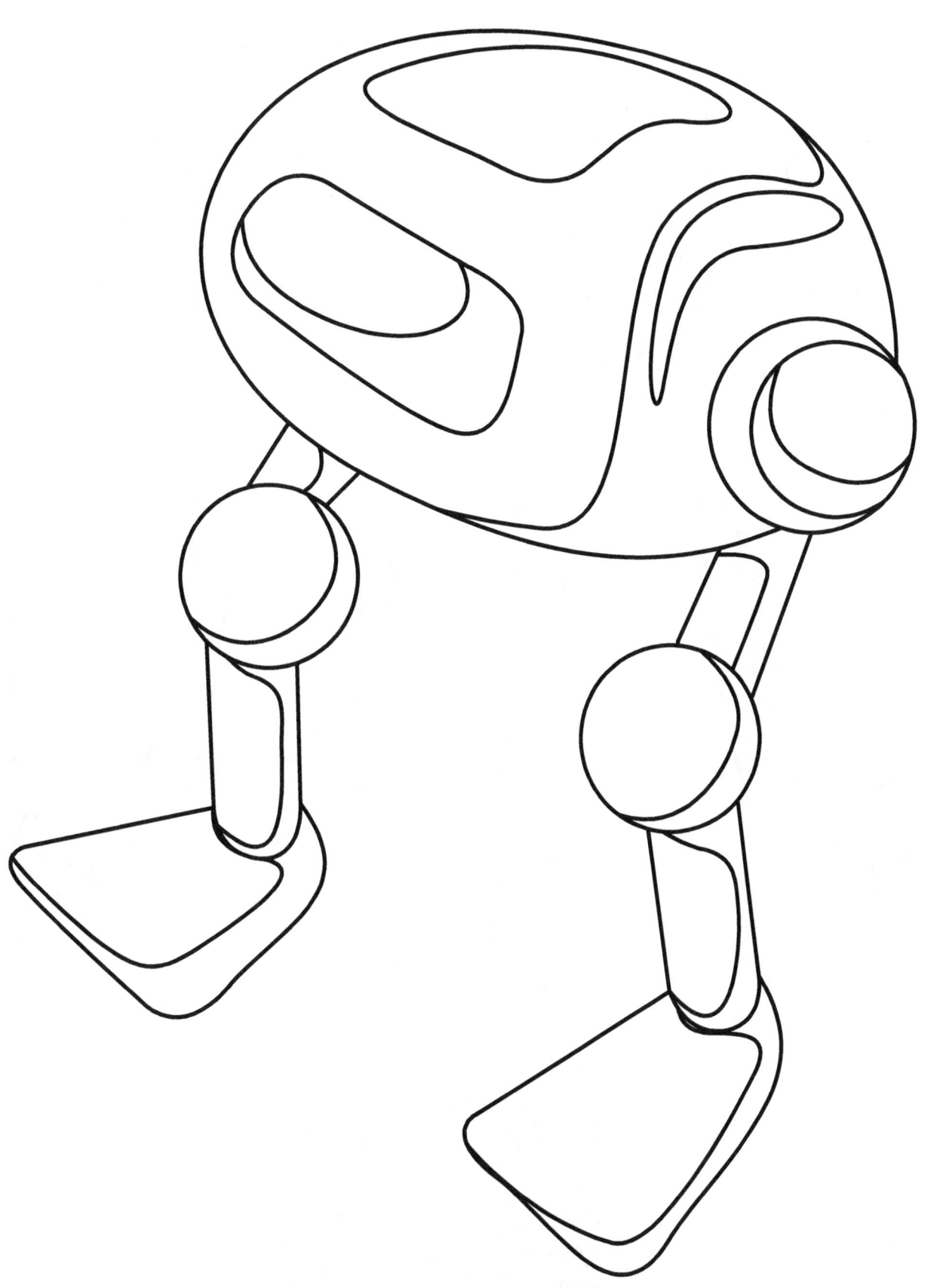

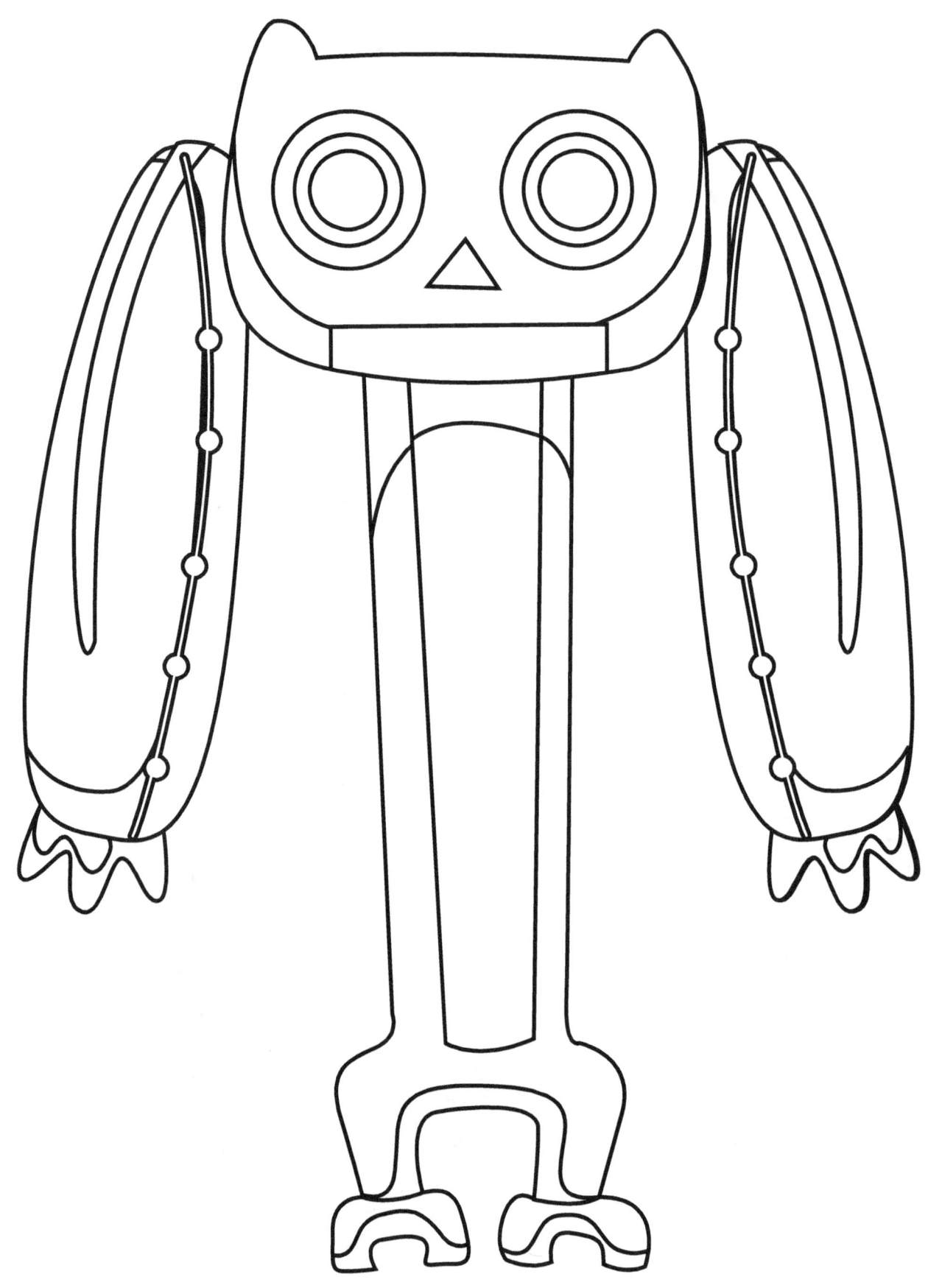

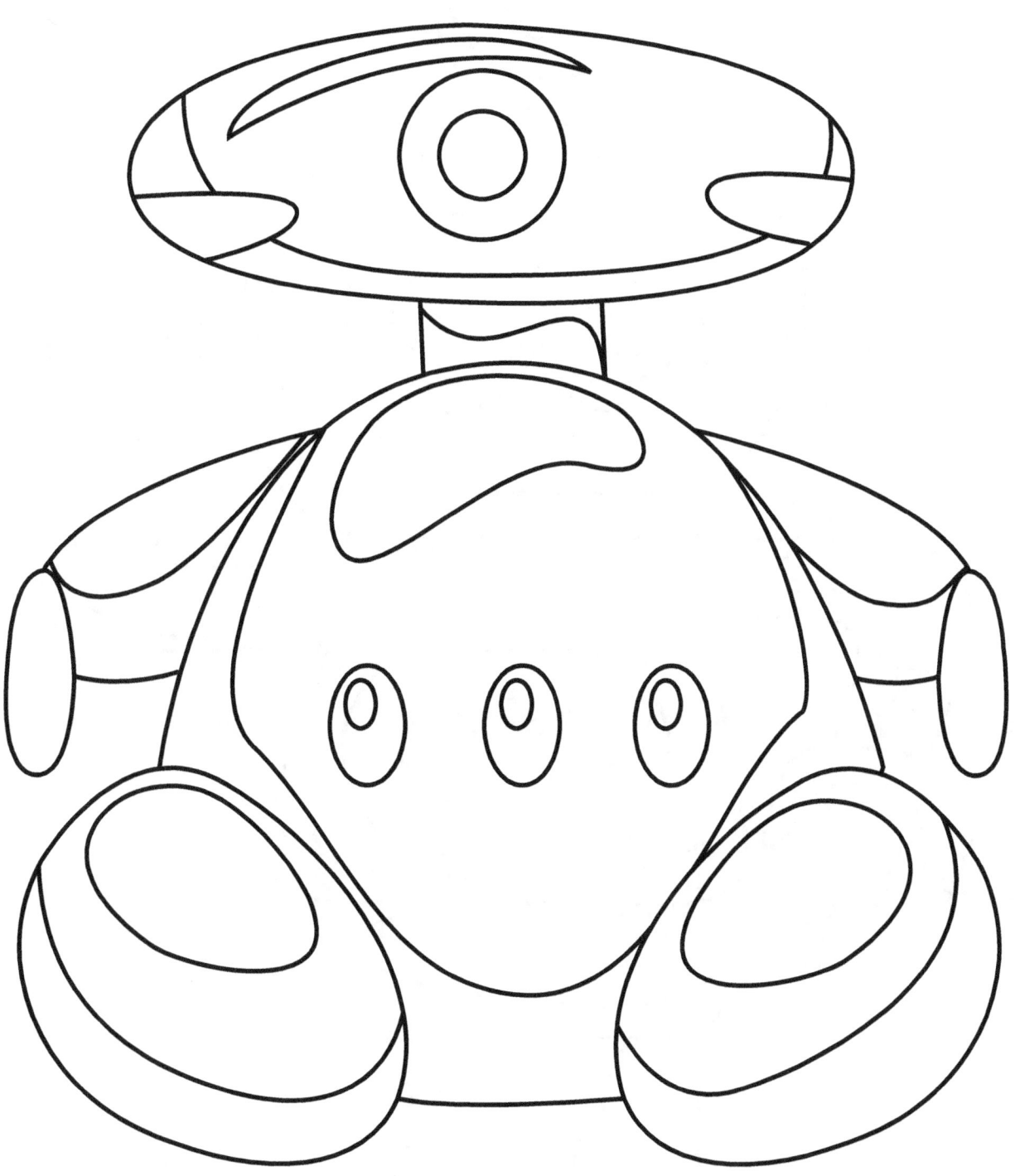

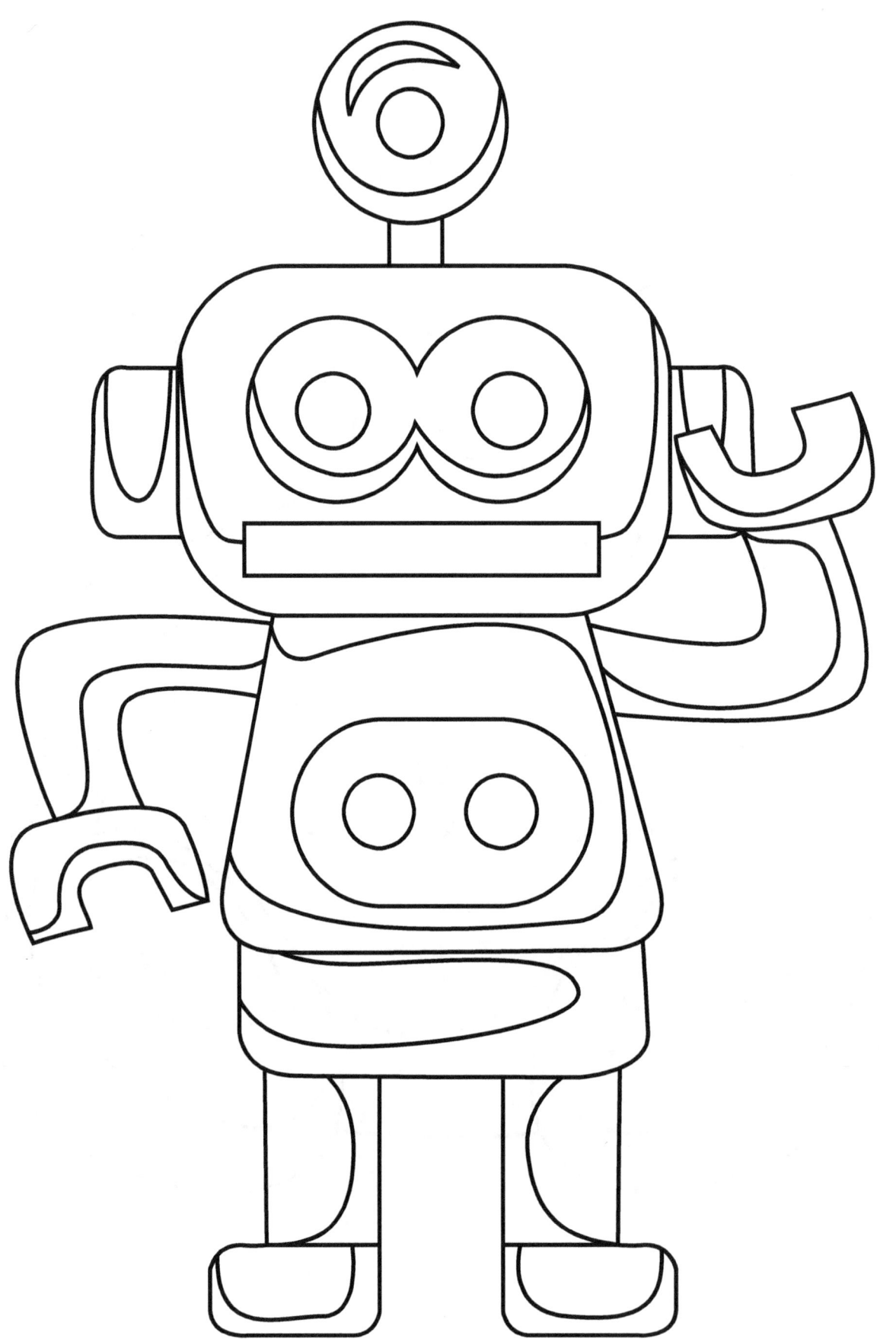

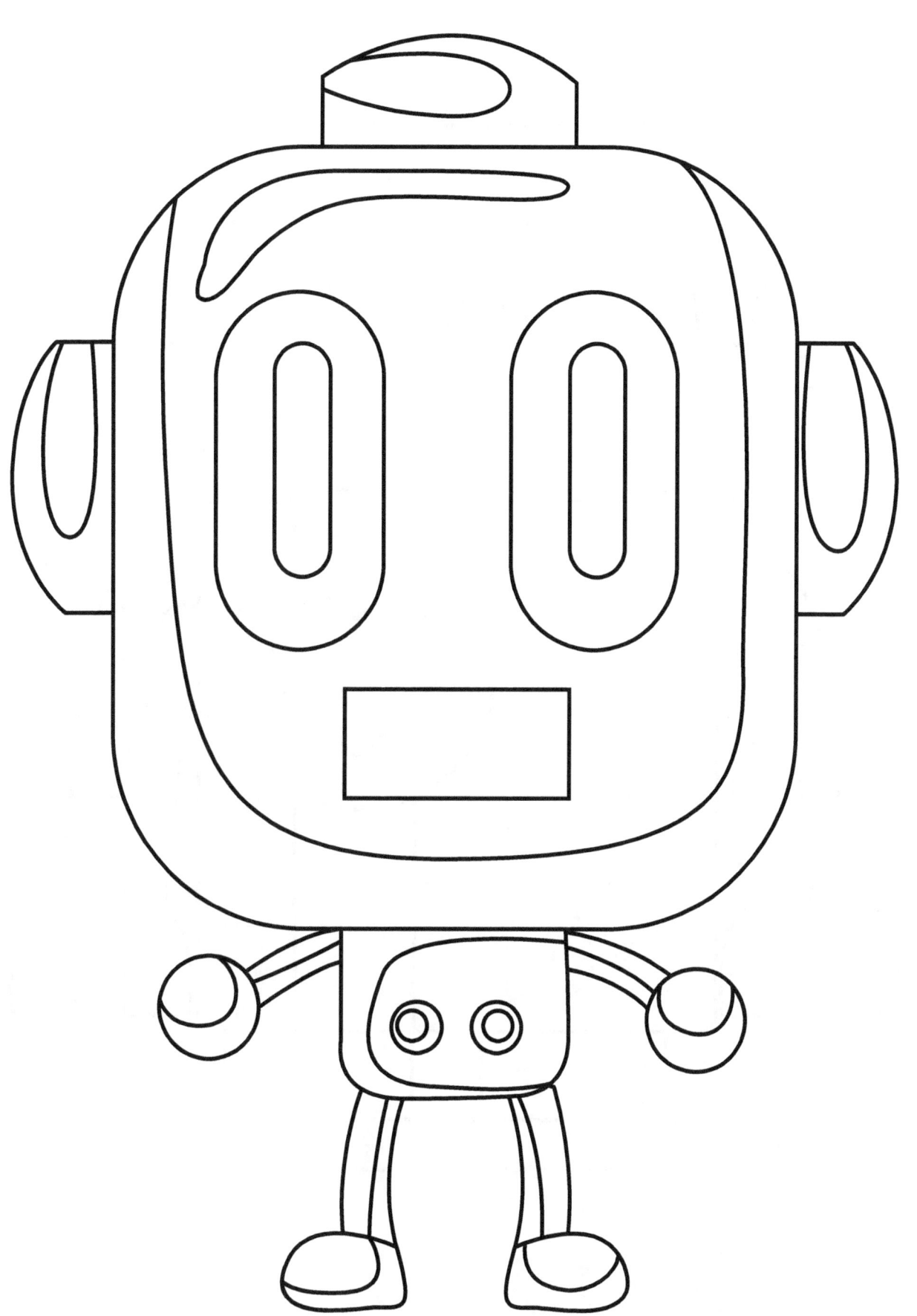

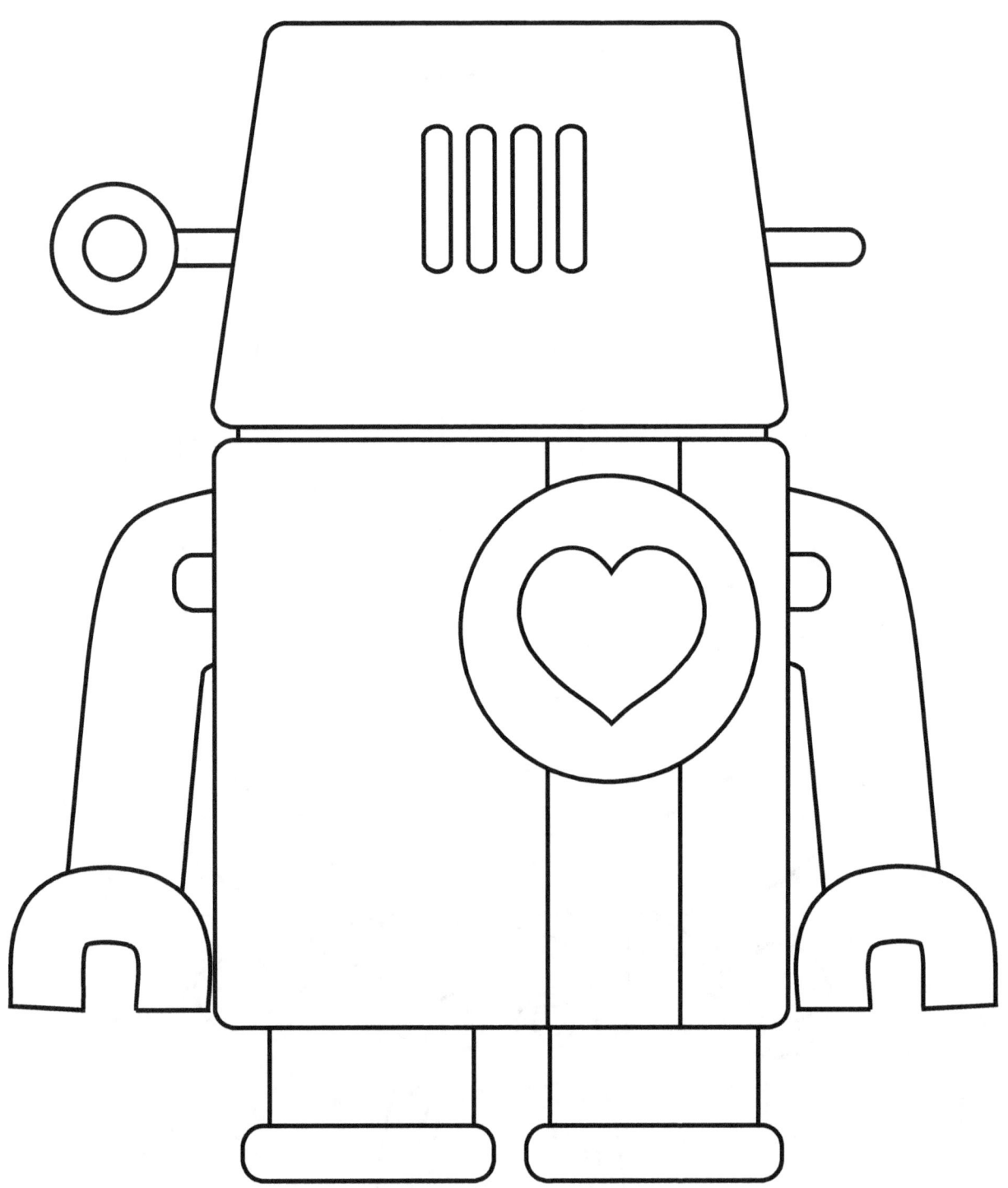

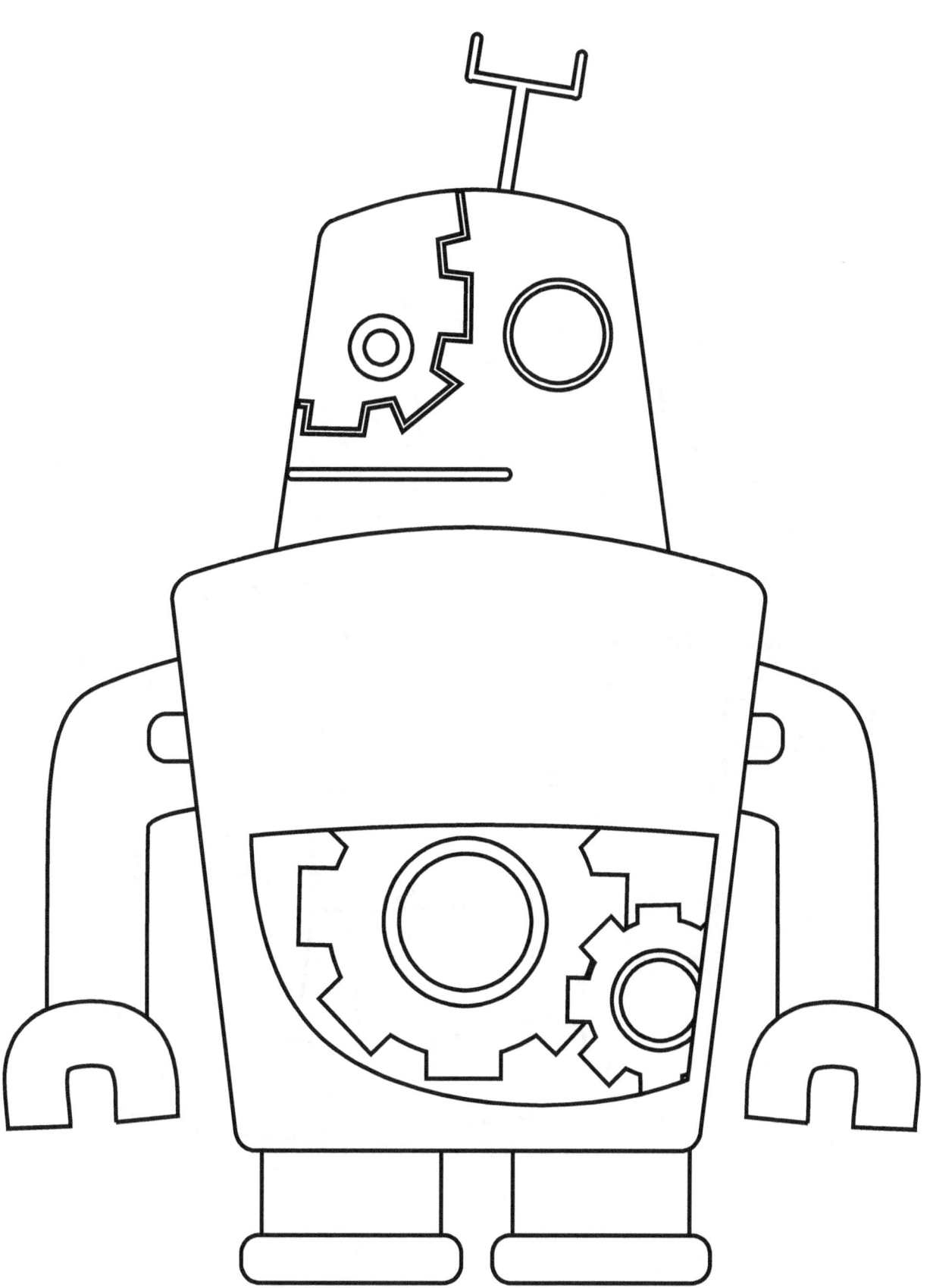

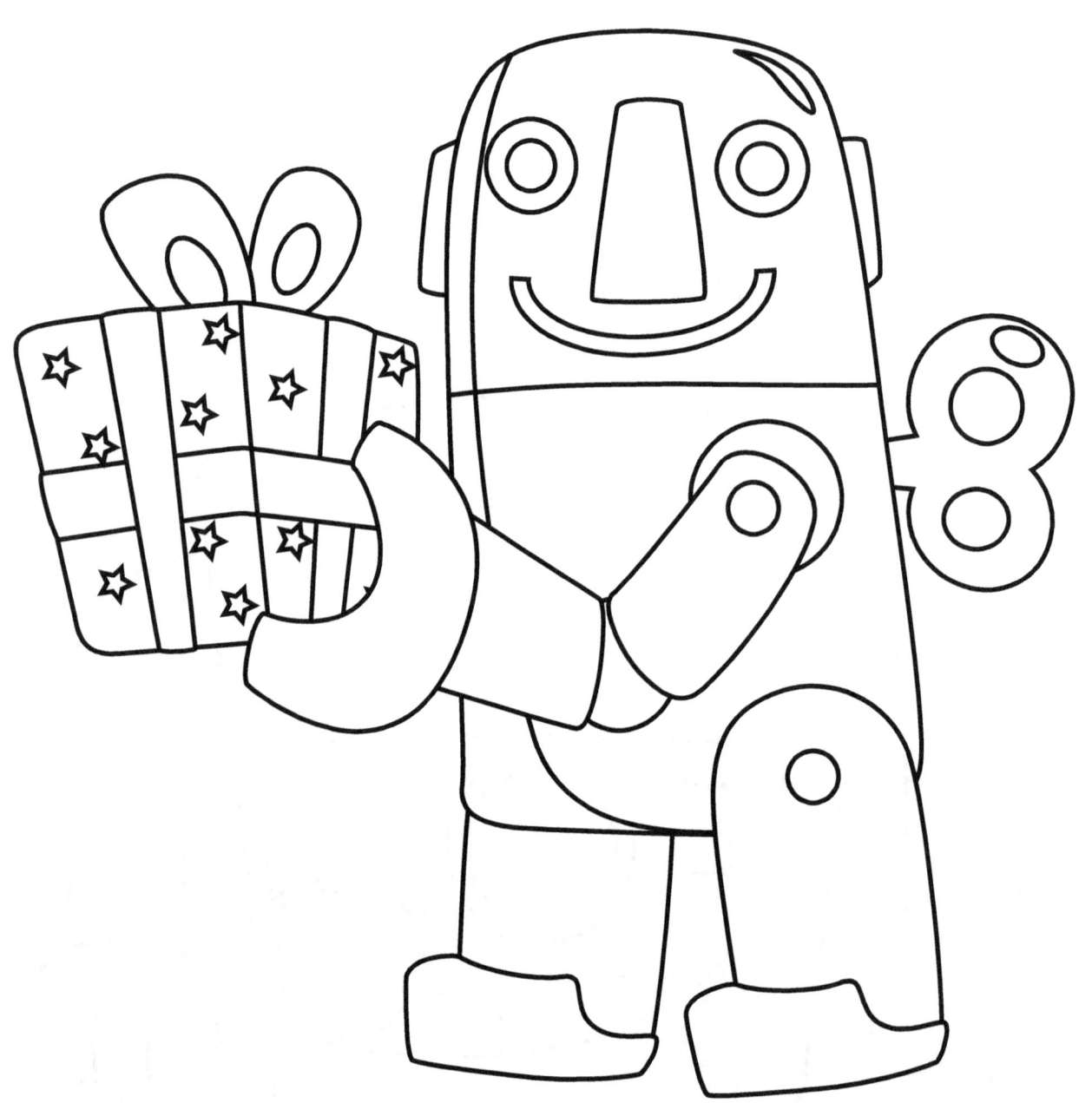

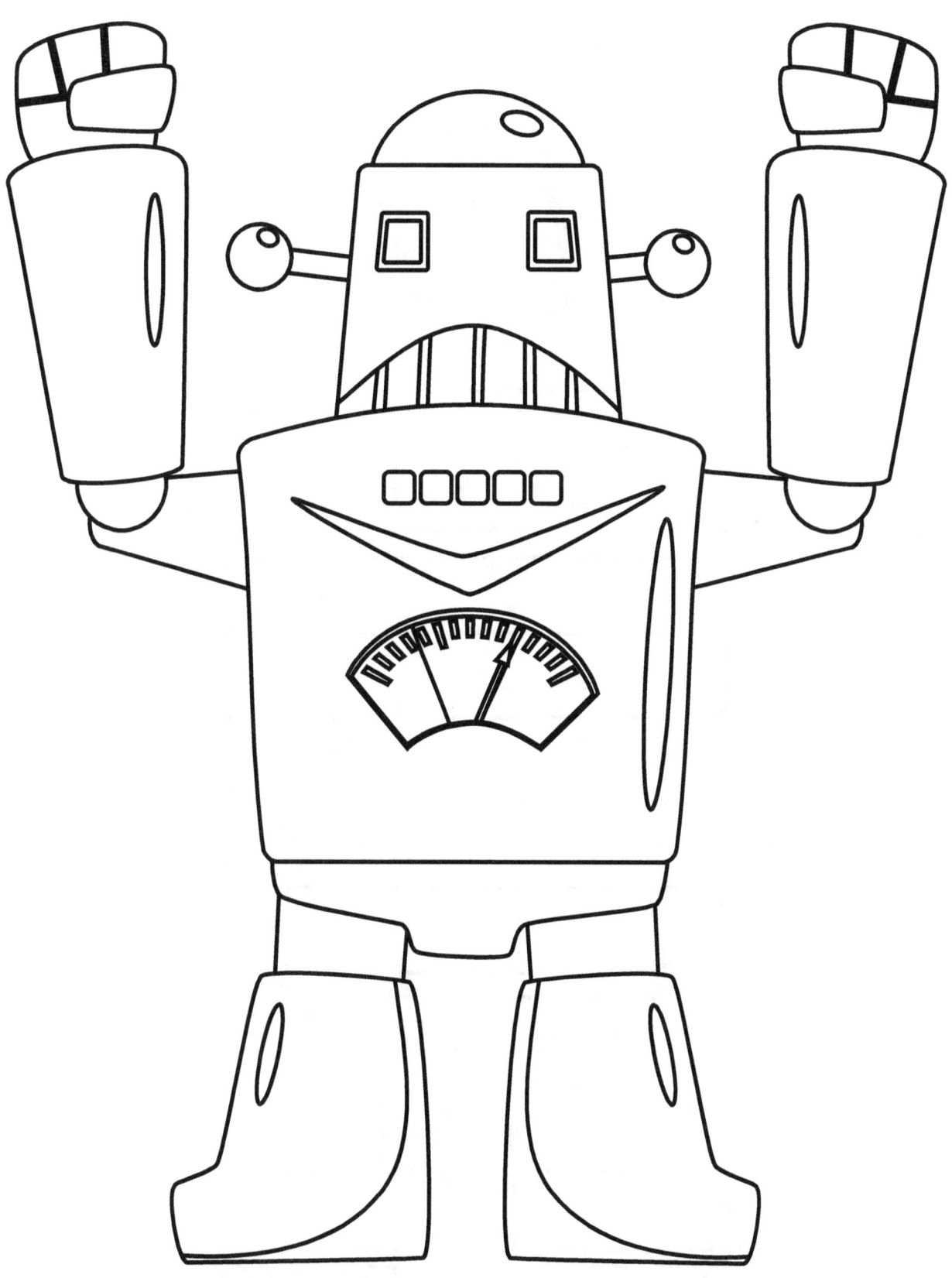

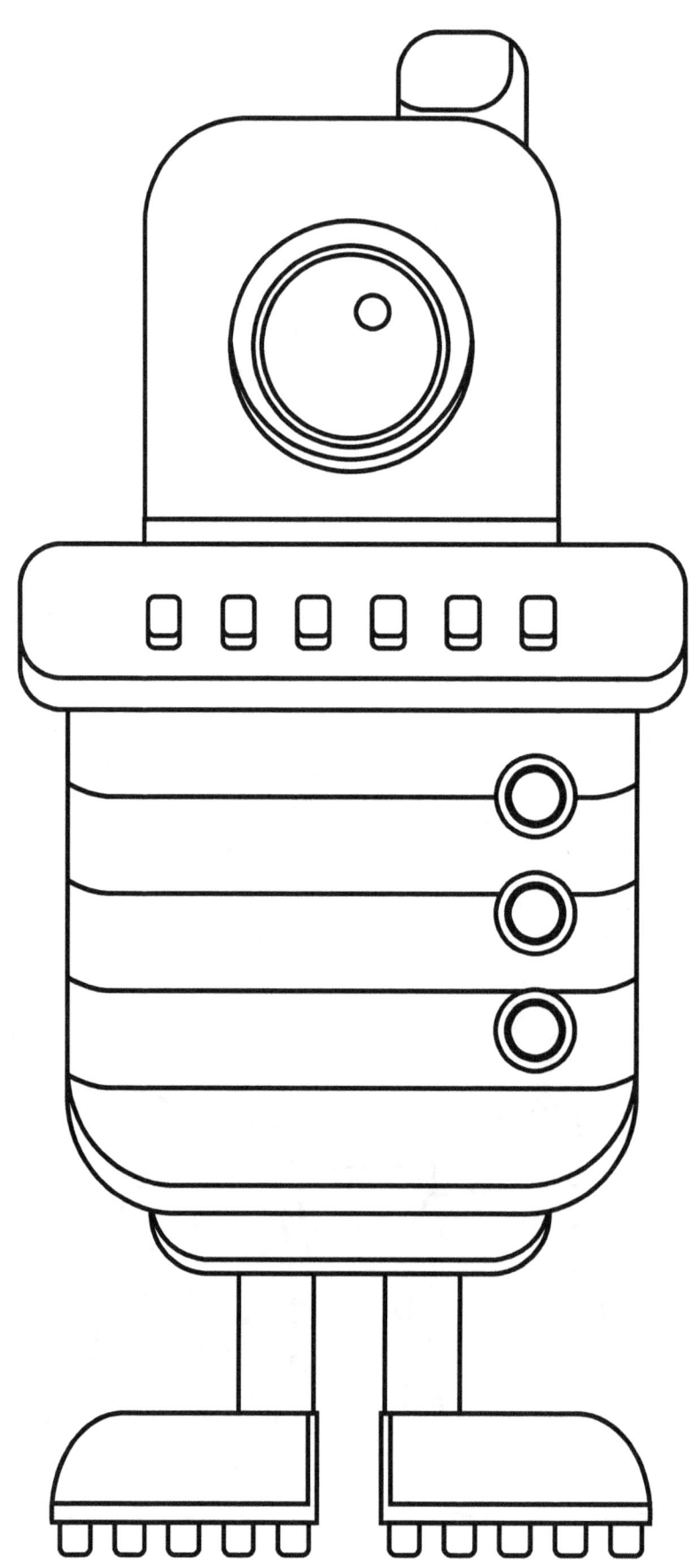

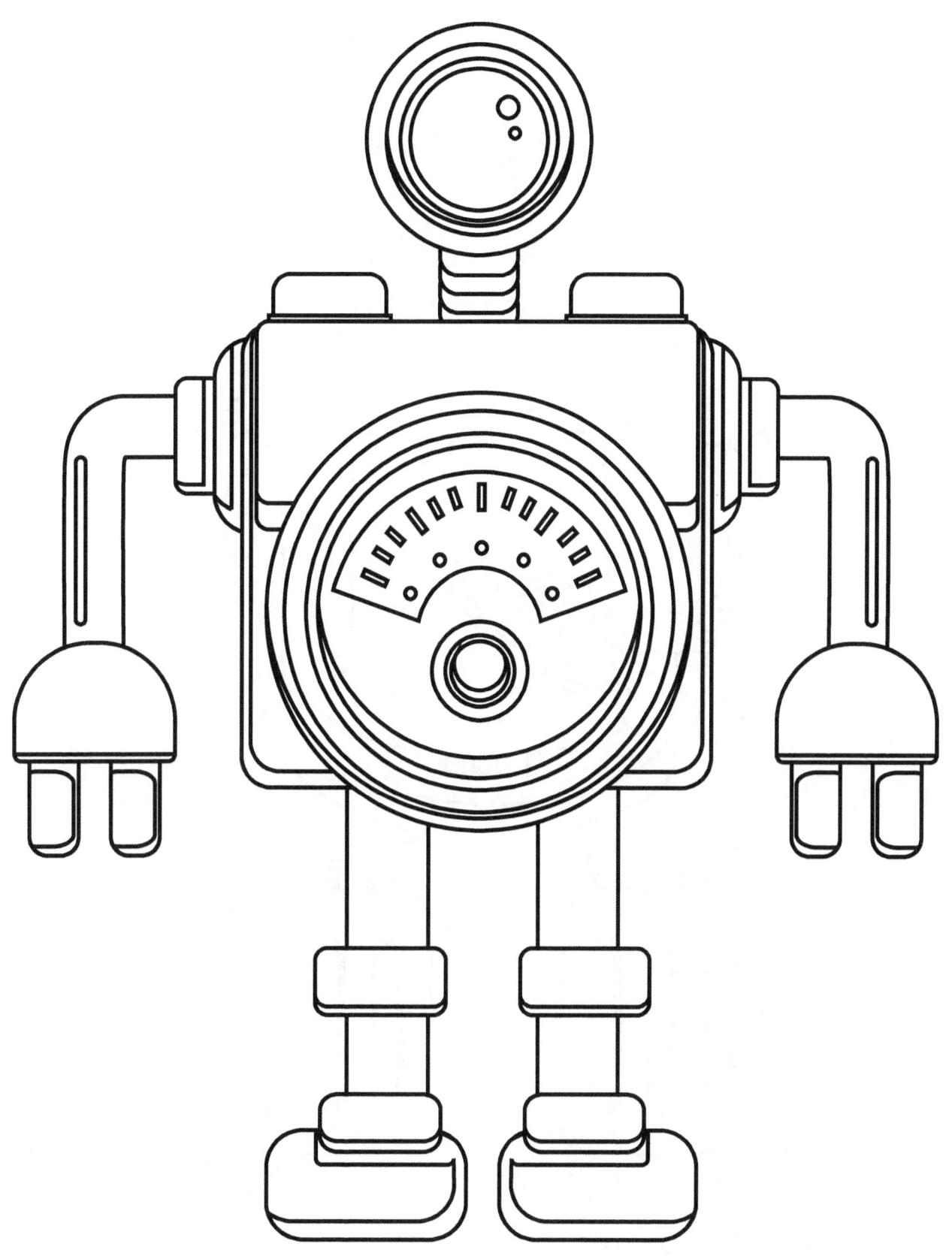

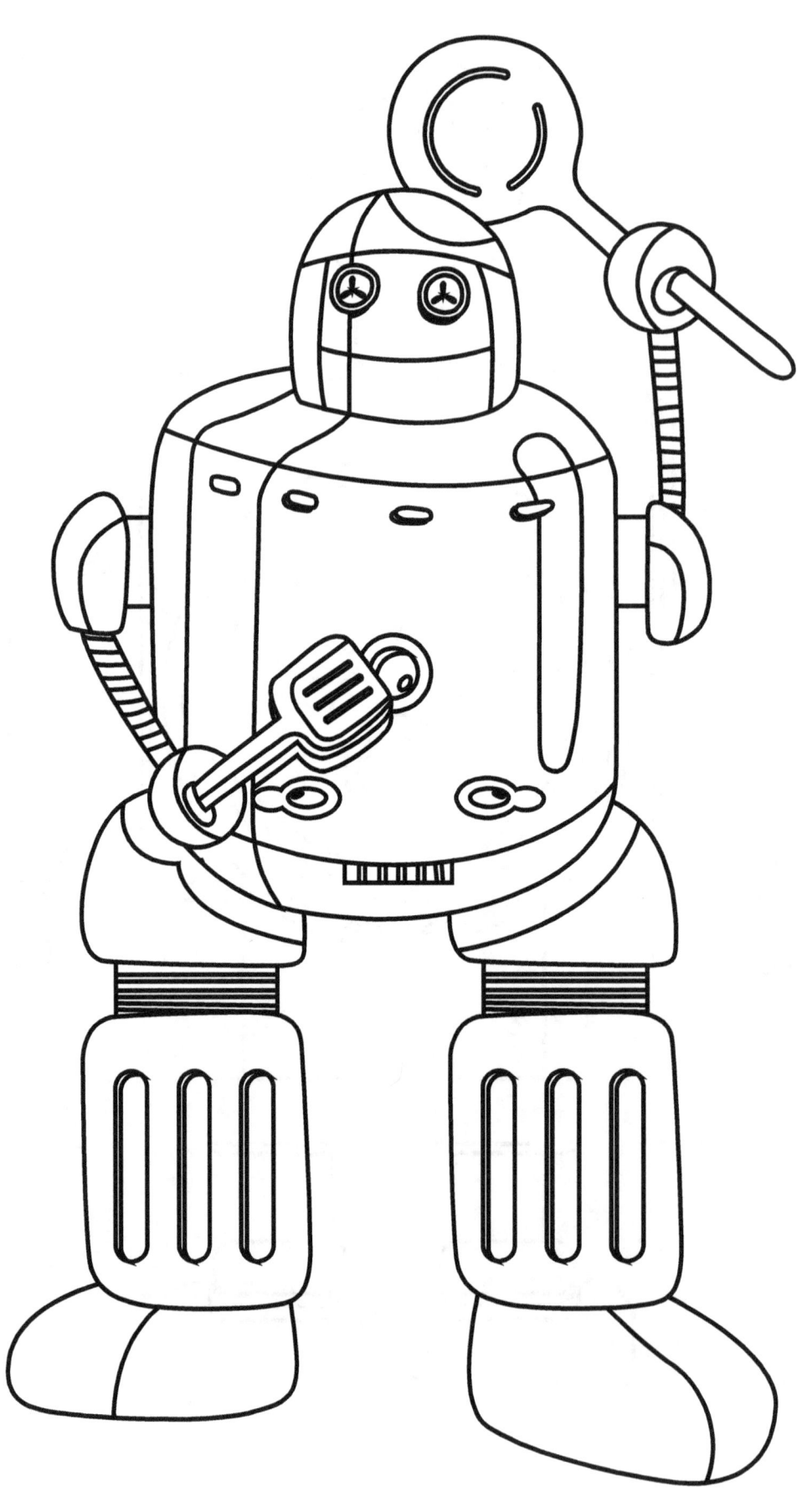

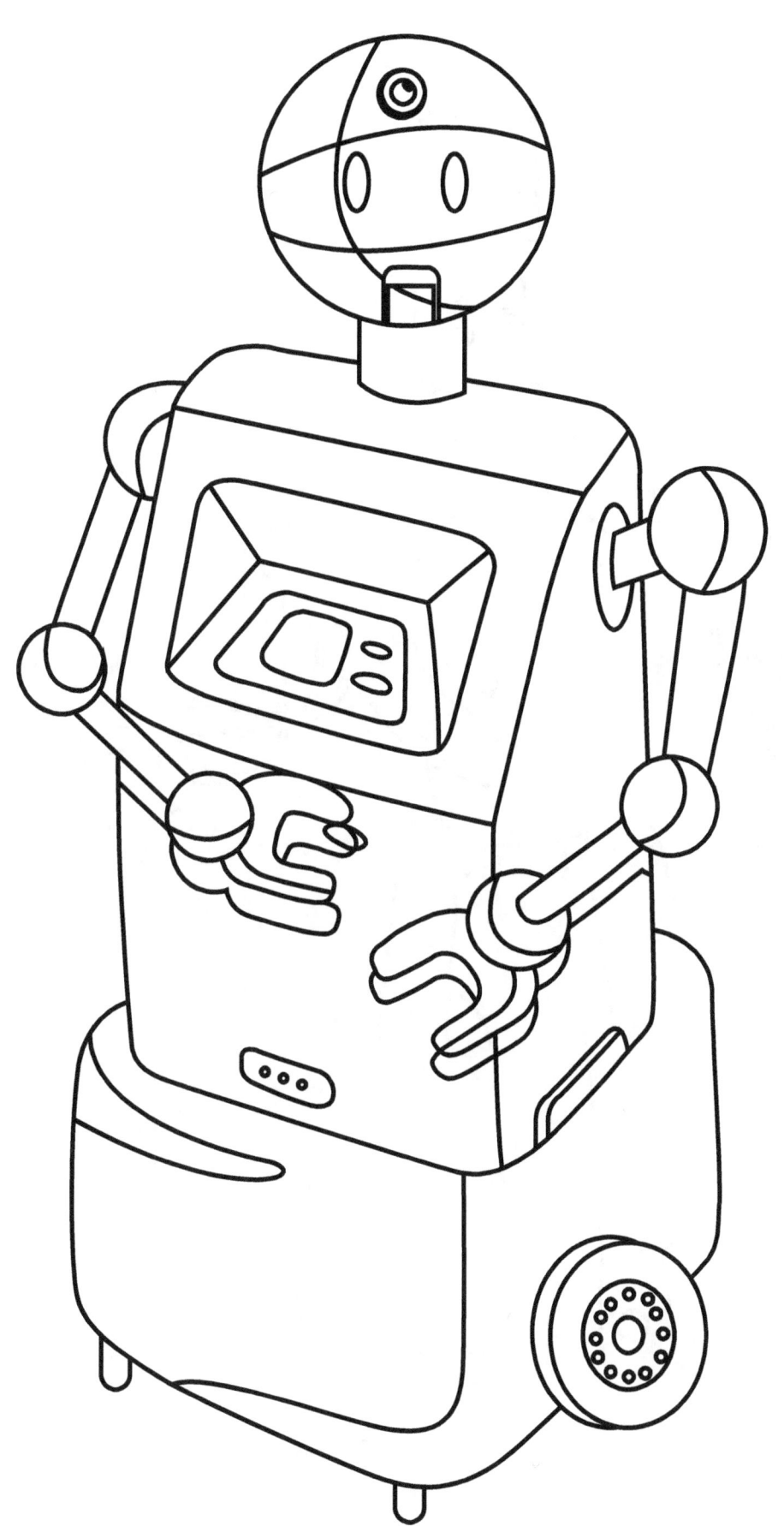

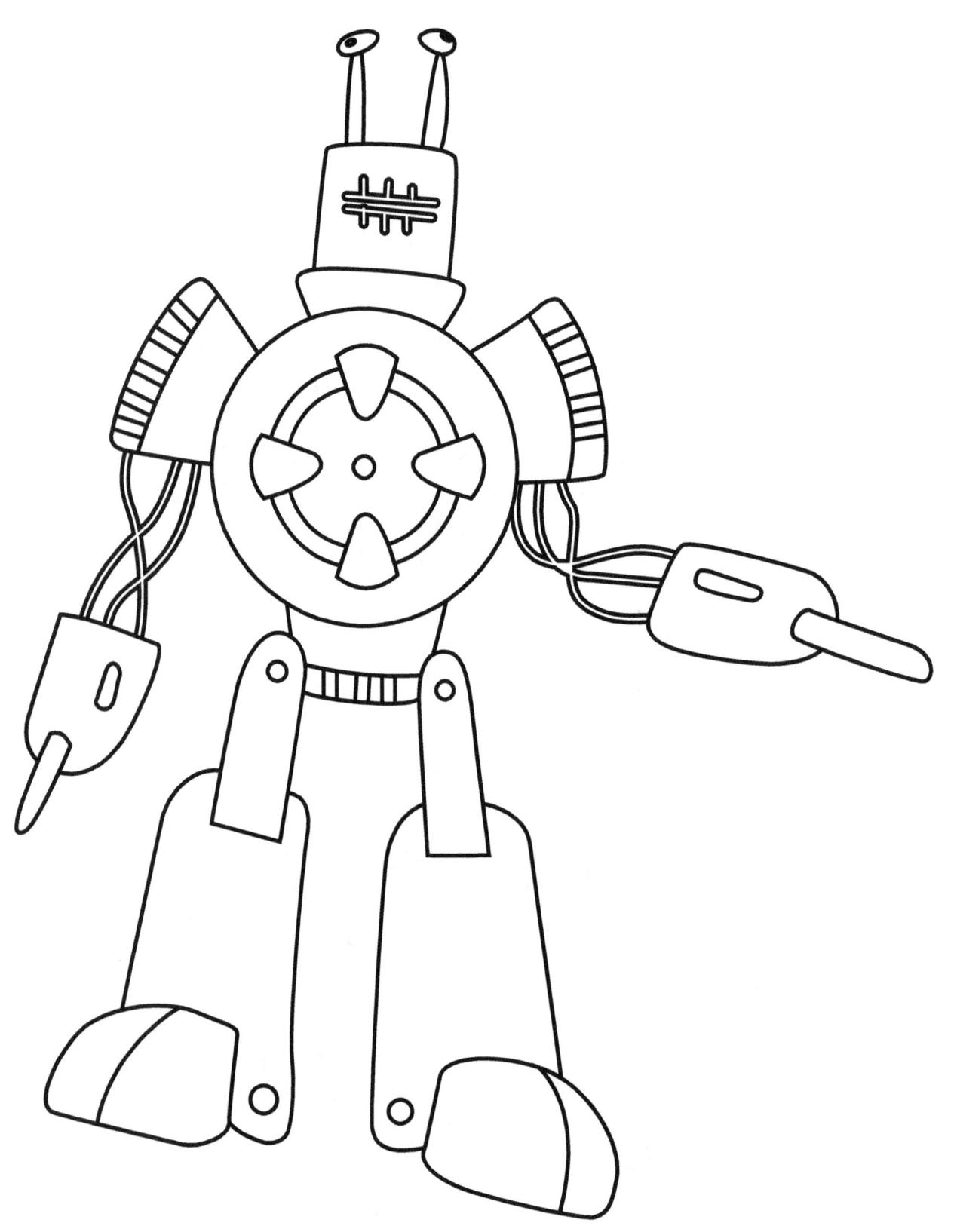

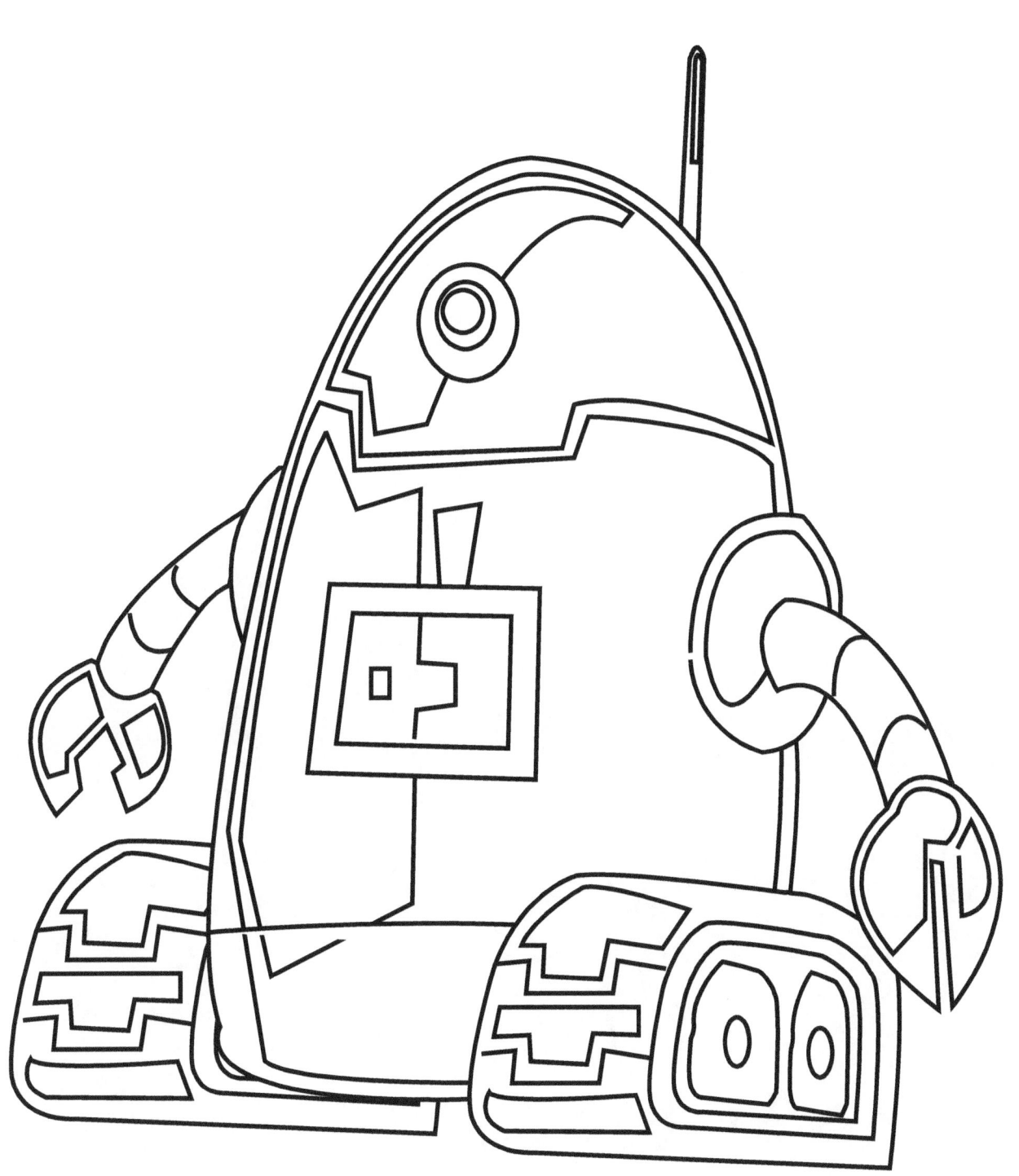